Biblical Foun

The New Way
of Living

by Larry Kreider

House To House Publications
Ephrata, Pennsylvania USA

The New Way of Living

Larry Kreider

Updated Edition © 2002, Reprinted 2003
Copyright © 1993, 1997, 1999
House to House Publications
1924 West Main Street, Ephrata, PA 17522
Telephone: (717) 738-3751
FAX: (717) 738-0656
Web site: www.dcfi.org

ISBN 1-886973-01-6
Design and illustrations by Sarah Mohler

Unless otherwise noted, all scripture quotations in this publication are taken from the *Holy Bible, New International Version* (NIV).
© 1973, 1978, 1984 by International Bible Society. Used by permission of Zondervan Publishing House. All rights reserved.

Biblical Foundations

CONTENTS

Books in this Series

This is the second book in a twelve-book series designed to help believers to build a solid biblical foundation in their lives.

A corresponding *Biblical Foundations for Children* book is also available (see page 63).

Introduction

The foundation of the Christian faith is built on Jesus Christ and His Word to us, the Holy Bible. This twelve-book *Biblical Foundation Series* includes elementary principles you need to help you lay a strong spiritual foundation in your life.

In this second Biblical Foundation book, *The New Way of Living,* we will look at two of the six foundational doctrines of the Christian faith found in Hebrews 6:1-2—**repentance from dead works and faith toward God**: *Therefore, leaving the discussion of the elementary principles of Christ, let us go on to perfection, not laying again the foundation of repentance from dead works and of faith toward God, of the doctrine of baptisms, of laying on of hands, of resurrection of the dead, and of eternal judgment (NKJ).* We will learn that we must repent from trying to gain God's acceptance by doing good things (Hebrews 6:2). Good deeds done to impress God or man are "dead works," and they do not get us closer to God. Only true repentance leads to faith in God.

In this book, the foundation truths from the Word of God are presented with modern day parables that help you easily understand the basics of Christianity. Use this book and the other 11 *Biblical Foundation* books to lay a solid spiritual foundation in your life, or if you are already a mature Christian, these books are great tools to assist you in discipling others. May His Word become life to you today.

God bless you!
Larry Kreider

How to Use This Resource

Personal study

Read from start to finish as an individual study program to build a firm Christian foundation and develop spiritual maturity.

- Each chapter has a key verse excellent to commit to memory.
- Additional scriptures in gray boxes are used for further study.
- Each reading includes questions for personal reflection and room to journal at the end of the book.

Daily devotional

Use as a devotional for a daily study of God's Word.

- Each chapter is divided into 7-day sections for weekly use.
- Additional days at the end of the book bring the total number of devotionals to one complete month. The complete set of 12 books gives one year's worth of daily devotionals.
- Additional scriptures are used for further study.
- Each day includes reflection questions and a place to write answers at the end of the book.

Mentoring relationship

Use for a spiritual parenting relationship to study, pray and discuss life applications together.

- A spiritual father or mother can easily take a spiritual son or daughter through these short Bible study lessons and use the reflection questions to provoke dialogue about what is learned.
- Read each day or an entire chapter at a time.

Small group study

Study this important biblical foundation in a small group setting.

- The teacher studies the material in the chapters and teaches, using the user-friendly outline provided at the end of the book.

Taught as a biblical foundation course

These teachings can be taught by a pastor or other Christian leader as a basic biblical foundation course.

- Students read an assigned portion of the material.
- In the class, the leader teaches the assigned material using the chapter outlines at the end of the book.

CHAPTER 1

Works Vs. Faith

KEY MEMORY VERSE

For it is by grace you have been saved,
through faith—and this not from yourselves,
it is the gift of God—not by works,
so that no one can boast.
Ephesians 2:8-9

An elementary principle: Repentance from dead works

After I received Jesus Christ as the Lord of my life, I realized I had to rebuild my life on a new foundation of the truths found in the Word of God. To grow in my Christian life, I first had to lay down elementary principles of Christianity. Only then could I build upon them to grow in greater maturity.

The spiritual building blocks to build into our lives are basic truths that are found in the Word of God. Starting with this book and continuing through books 3 and 4 in this 12-book *Biblical Foundation Series*, we will examine each of the six spiritual building blocks found in Hebrews 6:1-2. *Therefore, leaving the discussion of the elementary principles of Christ, let us go on to perfection, not laying again the foundation of repentance from dead works and of faith toward God, of the doctrine of baptisms, of laying on of hands, of resurrection of the dead, and of eternal judgment (NKJ).*

Here, we are urged to move on to maturity, after building on the elementary principles of 1) repentance from dead works 2) faith toward God 3) baptisms 4) laying on of hands 5) resurrection of the dead 6) eternal judgment. The six principles listed in these verses help us build a solid foundation in our spiritual lives.

In this book, we look at the first foundational stone listed here: "repentance from dead works and faith toward God." We will learn that true repentance always goes before true faith...*the foundation of repentance from dead works and of faith toward God...(Hebrews 6:1 NKJ).*

"Repenting from dead works" means we realize that all the good deeds we do will never get us to heaven. Salvation comes only through saving faith in the Lord Jesus Christ. People who hope they can "work" their way to heaven by doing good and avoiding wrong should know that the Bible tells us, *For whoever keeps the whole law and yet stumbles at just one point is guilty of breaking all of it (James 2:10).*

REFLECTION
Building a solid foundation in your Christian life involves understanding what six principles? What does "repentanc from dead works" mean?

The truth is that no one can keep the law of God because even if we stumble in one point (and we will because we have a sin nature), we are guilty. In other words, if I have sinned one time or a million times, I have broken the law. If an airplane crashes 500 feet from the runway or 500 miles from the runway, it still crashes and the casualties are devastating.

Nothing good you do will get you to heaven, but Christ will get you there!

True repentance or false repentance?

In Biblical Foundation 1, we already mentioned that repentance means to change our mind and our actions. Repentance is "an inner change of mind resulting in an outward turning around; to face and to move in a completely new direction."[1]

There is a godly sorrow that accompanies true repentance. We find ourselves truly sorry that our sin has grieved the heart of a holy God. This sorrow will produce true repentance; a willingness to change our actions. When we experience true repentance, we can enjoy the forgiveness and the freedom that Jesus gives us.

Repentance
Isaiah 55:6 7
Ezekiel 18:30-32
Acts 3:19; 17:30; 20:21

There is such a thing as *false repentance*, however. False repentance is *repenting for any other reason except that God is worthy of our complete obedience.* For example, children who are caught doing something wrong by their parents may regret they were caught without ever feeling sorry for disobeying their parents. This is false repentance, which in reality, is not repentance at all.

How many times have we been guilty of doing the same thing? If we are only sorry that "we got caught" instead of genuinely being sorry for grieving the heart of God, then we have not truly repented. That means we cannot experience God's forgiveness either. 2 Corinthians 7:10 tells us that *godly sorrow brings repentance that leads to salvation and leaves no regret, but worldly sorrow brings death.*

The Bible says that Judas, who betrayed Jesus, repented. But he did not experience true repentance. His "repentance" was only remorse and regret. He did not change his mind and direction like biblical repentance requires. In fact, after he felt terrible remorse, he went and hanged himself. He could no longer find a place of repentance. He could find no way to change his mind.

Just being sorry is not enough. We must trust God to completely change us inside. When we truly repent, Jesus' blood cleanses us from our sin and we can go on to live a new life in a new way. True repentance means that we realize we have sinned against a holy God and our inner change of mind results in a change in our direction.

Although God gives us salvation and forgiveness after true repentance, we may still suffer the consequences of our past sins. Broken relationships and families, loss of trust, sexual diseases, or bad habits are all examples of natural consequences of past sin. But the Lord promises to give us the strength to work through the consequences and to help us live victoriously (Philippians 4:13).

REFLECTION
What is the difference between tr
repentance and false repentance?
What must be your only reason fc
repenting?
What does godly sorrow lead to?

Sometimes we will also have to pay a price for our past sin. For example, a man guilty of murder who later comes to Christ is forgiven of his sin by God, but he still has to pay a price for the consequences of his actions. His sorrow and repentance will not keep him from serving a prison sentence for his crime.

[1] Derek Prince, The Spirit-Filled Believers Handbook (Lake Mary, FL: Creation House, 1993), p. 101.

Good works vs. dead works

Now that we understand the *repentance* part of *repentance from dead works*, what are "dead works?" Our works refer to good deeds or good things that we do. A dead work is any work, or good deed, that we do to try to earn favor with God. No amount of human goodness, human works, human morality, or religious activity can gain acceptance with God or get anyone into heaven.

People in certain parts of Malaysia perform a peculiar ritual to appease their gods and try to gain favor with them. Every year they choose one young man from their tribe and sink hooks into the flesh of his back. Then a rope is attached to the hooks in the young man's back and a cart loaded with a one-foot-high statue of the local god. The people believe they can gain right standing with their god when the blood-covered young man pulls the idol and cart through their town.

This may sound like a strange and senseless thing for someone to do, yet we are doing a similar thing when we trust in our good works to try to please God. The devil has his hooks in our minds, making us believe that we are accepted by the Lord because of the good things we do. This is entirely wrong thinking and in opposition to what God's Word says in Ephesians 2:8-9. *For it is by grace you have been saved, through faith—and this not from yourselves, it is the gift of God—not by works, so that no one can boast.*

We have been saved through faith. We have favor with God because we have placed our trust in the person and work of Christ. Only Jesus Christ gives us real life. Works are totally incapable of producing spiritual life in us. And yet, we can get caught in the trap of trying to win God's favor by our works. These actions are dead works.

Paul, the apostle, chided the Galatian Christians because they had started out by faith in Christ, but were now trying, through religious dead works, to gain spirituality. *You foolish Galatians! Who has bewitched you? ...Did you receive the Spirit by observing the law, or by believing what you heard? Are you so foolish? After beginning with the Spirit, are you now trying to attain your goal by human effort? ...Does God give you his Spirit and work miracles among you because you observe the law, or because you believe what you heard? (Galatians 3:1-3,5).*

Dead works can be very religious. If Christians place their faith in their witnessing, or their Bible reading, or attending their church meetings, instead of putting their faith in God, these good deeds become dead works. Involvement in the church, helping the poor, giving offerings, being a good husband or wife, being an obedient child— all these can be dead works if we are trying to gain favor with God through doing them.

I have met people who think that if they break their bad habits, God will accept them. They say, "I'll stop smoking, and then God will accept me." God does not accept us because we have overcome a bad habit. He accepts us because His Son, Jesus Christ, died on the cross two thousand years ago for our sins, and when we receive Him, we become His sons and daughters. When we give our lives to Jesus, He will give us the power and grace to stop smoking or discontinue

REFLECTION
In efforts of trying to gain favor with God, what are some "dead works" people perform?
How can you know your works are good and not dead?

any other habit that does not bring glory to God. But He accepts us as we are and gives us the grace and desire to change.

Our goodness does not bring us favor with God. We already have favor with God! God has called us to do good works, but we do them because we already have His favor, not to gain His favor.

The futility of our works to save us

So now we know that good works are powerless to help us through the pearly gates of heaven. The Bible tells us that even the best "good works" we do to please God are like filthy rags compared to His goodness. *...All our righteous acts are like filthy rags... (Isaiah 64:6).*

That is why any good deed done to impress God or man is a "dead work." There's a story that is told about a beggar who was walking down the road one day when he saw the king approaching with his entourage. The beggar was awestruck. Then the king looked down on the beggar and said, "Come, sit on my horse with me." The beggar was astounded. "Why would the king do such a thing?" he wondered.

The beggar laid his questions aside and mounted the king's horse. They rode to the palace together and as they entered the royal residence, the king said to the beggar, "Today I have chosen you to live in my palace. I'm going to give you new garments to wear and all of the sumptuous food that you can eat. I will make sure that all of your needs are met."

The beggar thought for a moment. All that he had to do was to receive from the king what he had promised to give him. This was too good to be true. He didn't deserve this royal treatment. It just did not make sense. How could the king accept him and meet all of his needs when he had done nothing to deserve it?

From that time on, the beggar lived by the king's provision. However, the beggar thought, "I think I should hang onto my old clothes just in case the king doesn't really mean what he said. I don't want to take any chances." So, the beggar hung onto his old rags...just in case.

When the beggar was old and dying, the king came to his bedside. When the monarch glanced down and saw the old rags still clutched in the beggar's hand, both men began to weep. The beggar finally realized that even though he had lived his whole life with the king in a royal palace, he had never really trusted the king. Instead, He had chosen to live his entire life under a cruel deception. He should have lived like a royal prince.

Many of us do the same thing. We give our lives to Jesus, but we insist on hanging onto and trusting in our works and the good things we do, "just in case." However, trusting these "dead works," instead of placing our entire confidence in Jesus Christ, is like hanging onto filthy rags from God's perspective. The Lord does not receive us because of our good works. No, we're received by God only because of faith in His Son Jesus Christ and what He has done

REFLECTION
Examine yourself—are you hanging onto some ragged dead works "just in case"? On what condition does God accept you?

for us on the cross. We are righteous by faith in Him. Let's not get caught, at the end of our lives, clinging to our old rags, because somehow we found it too hard to believe that the Lord desires to bless us and fill us with His life, even though we do not deserve it at all.

God's perspective on good works

DAY 5

Should we do good works, then? Yes, absolutely! God wants us to do good works. We show our love by actions! We should do millions of good works in our lifetime, but only because God loves us and has accepted us already; we cannot try to earn His favor. Works play no part at all in securing salvation. But after we reach out to the Lord in faith and know that He accepts us and loves us just the way we are, we will find ourselves wanting to obey God. We will want to do good works because God has changed us. Paul told the Ephesians, *For we are God's workmanship, created in Christ Jesus to do good works, which God prepared in advance for us to do (Ephesians 2:10).*

God empowers us to live the Christian life so we will want to act on the great love He has bestowed on us! I don't take care of my children so I can be their father; I take care of my children because I am their father and love them deeply. We don't do good works because we want to become righteous; we do good works because we are righteous.

I once read a story about an eight year old boy who was instructed by his mother to hoe the family garden. His mother told him to hoe two rows of beans. She showed him exactly how she wanted him to do it, and told him, "Now, when you get through, tell me so I can come and look it over." When he finally finished according to her instructions, he called her to inspect it. She took one look at it and shook her head in disapproval, "Well, son, it looks like you're going to have to redo this. For most boys this would be all right. But you are not most boys: you are my son. And my son can do better than this!" Did his mother stop loving him because he did not hoe the garden to perfection? No. She simply expected that he could do better. God's life in us produces good works and changed character. His love for us motivates us to want to reach out to others and do good works for the right reasons— because we love Him with all our hearts.

REFLECTION
If your own good works are not pleasing to God, how do you explain Ephesians 2:10? Why does God expect good works from you? What must be your only motivation for doing good works?

DAY 6

True righteousness

In Romans 10:2-3, we read about some religious people who had zeal for God, but were trying to gain their salvation by their own merits. They were trying to establish their own righteousness, or *right standing* with God on their own terms. *For I can testify about them that they are zealous for God, but their zeal is not based on knowledge. Since they did not know the righteousness that comes from God and sought to establish their own, they did not submit to God's righteousness.*

These people did not know God's method of saving sinners. They did not realize they are saved only through faith in Jesus Christ. Instead, they tried to establish their own righteousness. They were sincere in their efforts, but sincerely wrong.

This reminds me of the young football player who finally caught the ball and took off with a great burst of speed—toward the other team's goal. This young man had zeal, and he ran as fast as he could, but he was headed in the wrong direction! He had misdirected zeal. Our zeal is misdirected if it is not founded on correct views of truth. Our good works cannot obtain favor with the Lord.

Once, when I was in a Latin American country with a friend, we needed to pay with pesos to get our flight out of the country. We didn't have pesos, so we offered them American dollars which were worth more than the pesos. No matter how hard we tried, they would not accept them. The government had set up their monetary system on pesos and we were using the wrong system. We had zeal, but our way didn't work.

REFLECTION
How do people try to establish their own righteousness? How can you know your "zeal for God" does not result in dead works?

We must be more than sincere: we must know the truth. We have to yield our hearts to Jesus Christ. Right standing with God only comes through faith in Jesus Christ. Satan will tempt us to trust in something—anything—other than the finished work of Jesus Christ for our salvation. Some people accept Jesus as Lord but add on all kinds of good works with hopes of becoming more righteous. God does not accept us because we eat the right foods, read the Bible in the right way, pray the right way or dress the right way. Our acceptance is in Jesus, period! We may do some of the above-mentioned good works, but we do not do them in order to be accepted by the Lord. We do them because we *have* been accepted!

What is like a pile of rubbish?

DAY 7

Paul, the apostle, was of pure Jewish descent, had a prestigious Greek education, and was one of the most influential interpreters of Christ's message and teaching as an early Christian missionary. But he considered all the knowledge and the great things he had done as a pile of garbage compared to knowing Jesus Christ. Paul says in Philippians 3:7-8, *But whatever was to my profit I now consider loss for the sake of Christ. What is more, I consider everything a loss compared to the surpassing greatness of knowing Christ Jesus my Lord, for whose sake I have lost all things. I consider them rubbish, that I may gain Christ.*

Those who trust in their Christian background or training or credentials to make themselves acceptable to God are trusting in the wrong things. If you grew up in a good Christian home and had the opportunity to get Bible training, thank God for it! However, even these good things are rubbish compared to knowing Jesus as Lord and trusting in His righteousness.

Knowing Christ and having an intimate relationship with Him is much more important than what we do or have done for Him. I am thankful that my wife cooks my meals and washes my clothes, but these good works mean nothing compared to our love relationship together. I just enjoy knowing her most of all. The same principle applies to our relationship with Jesus.

REFLECTION

Name some things Paul, the apostle, calls "rubbish" that we often trust instead of trusting in God's righteousness.
Is knowing Jesus personally the most important thing in your life?

If you have been trusting your good works or your background more than your relationship with Jesus, you can repent now. Jesus will fill you with His love, and you will experience His righteousness and His acceptance.

When we repent, we do an "about face"—we are sharply turned around! If we move from one geographical area to another, we need to change schools or change jobs. We go from one to another. True repentance always goes before true faith. So then, in our spiritual lives, we must repent of placing our faith in dead works and do an "about face" by placing our faith in the living God alone!

Faith
in God

An elementary principle: Faith toward God

In the previous chapter, we learned that we must repent from trying to gain God's acceptance by doing good things (Hebrews 6:2). Good deeds done to impress God or man are "dead works," and they do not get us closer to God. Only true repentance leads to faith in God.

The second part of the verse in Hebrews says that after repentance, we must move on to "faith toward God." Placing our faith in God is another elementary, foundational principle of our Christian lives. *Therefore, leaving the discussion of the elementary principles of Christ, let us go on to perfection, not laying again the foundation of...faith toward God...(Hebrews 6:1 NKJ).*

Faith
Acts 20:21
Hebrews 10:22; 11:7; 11:13
Romans 8:24-25; 2 Corinthians 5:17
1 Peter 1:8; John 20:29

What is faith? It is something that happens in the heart that produces a transformation in our lives. We cannot just make a profession of Christ in the realm of our minds. Faith toward God produces a change in our hearts. We are moved out of our sin and into His righteousness by our faith. The Bible literally defines *faith* in Hebrews 11:1 when it says, *Now faith is being sure of what we hope for and certain of what we do not see.*

Faith involves believing first and then seeing. As Christians, we live and act as if we have already seen the Lord because we have confidence in God—we have placed our faith in Him. But of course, God is not visible to the naked eye. He is visible only to the eye of faith. We believe even though we do not "see" in the physical sense.

God called Abraham "a father of many nations" long before he had a son. The Bible says that Abraham "in hope believed" (Romans 4:18) that this promise would come to pass. He did not wait until he saw the physical evidence before he believed by faith.

REFLECTION
What does faith produce?
According to Romans 12:3, where does faith come from?

Faith is a "gift of God" (Ephesians 2:8) and God uses His divine spoon to give you a "measure of faith" according to Romans 12:3...*in accordance with the measure of faith God has given you.*

Therefore, the question is not, "How do I get faith?" but, "How do I exercise the faith that God has already given me?" All of us have faith in something. We may have faith in our ability to drive our car or faith that the ceiling in our home will not fall down. Some people have faith in their abilities, while others have faith in their philosophies. As Christians, our faith must be focused exclusively on the living God—in Jesus Christ.

DAY 2

We receive Jesus by faith alone

How do we receive Christ as Lord? By faith. How do we live out our Christian life each day? By faith. Hebrews 11:6 tells us, *and without faith it is impossible to please God, because anyone who comes to him must believe that he exists and that he rewards those who earnestly seek him.*

Faith is our first response to God. We put our trust in Christ by faith and faith alone. We cannot depend on *our* abilities. We must depend on *His* abilities. If the world-renowned evangelist, Billy Graham, depended on his own works to be in right standing with God, he'd never make it, because God's standard is perfection. You see, even a great man of God like Billy Graham has not been perfect. No one is

> **Justification by faith alone**
> Galatians 2:16;3:11;5:4-5
> Romans 5:1

perfect except Jesus Christ. That's why we have to repent from trying to gain acceptance from God by our own morality or good works. Our efforts to "try harder" at being a better student, a better spouse, or a stronger Christian witness can never gain for us more acceptance from God. Placing our faith in God is the only way to please Him. We place our faith in the living God and serve Him for one reason, *because He is God.* He is worthy of our praise and our complete allegiance.

Since we have embraced Christ by faith, we must hold fast and not be sidetracked. When we receive Jesus as our Lord and put our faith in Him, we find that our lives are no longer filled solely with our own thoughts and de-

REFLECTION
How can you please God? How can Christ live in you and you in Him? In what ways is Christ living in you?

sires, as our lives had been before we came to Christ. Things have changed! Christ is now actually living in us. Galatians 2:20 says... *Christ lives in me. The life I live in the body, I live by faith in the Son of God, who loved me and gave himself for me.*

Why is this so important? Because when I realize that Christ lives in me, I begin to see life from a different perspective. I see it as it really is. Christ lives in me. And the same Holy Spirit that dwelt in Jesus Christ two thousand years ago, that gave Him the power to live a supernatural life, is also in me enabling me to live a supernatural life. His power will lead me on.

DAY 3

Put yourself to the test

Remember, faith is not based on our outward appearance or on what we do, although true faith will result in changed behavior. We may be church members, give money in the offering every week, help other people and even give our lives in service to others. But, as we learned earlier, these good works do not make a person a true Christian, although a Christian will certainly do such things. People who look like Christians on the outside, but have no real spiritual life on the inside, are disappointing counterfeits.

The Holy Spirit guides us in truth
John 14:17; Psalms 25:5
John 14:26

Sometimes counterfeit Christians and genuine Christians look so much alike on the outside that you can hardly tell the difference. God wants us to take stock of our own lives to be completely sure that we are genuine. The scriptures tell us, *Examine yourselves to see whether you are in the faith; test yourselves. Do you not realize that Christ Jesus is in you—unless, of course, you fail the test? (2 Corinthians 13:5).*

We must look closely at ourselves and compare what we are to what the scriptures say a Christian must be. Police officers who are trained to spot counterfeit money spend much time in training and studying the real thing. When we study the real thing, the Bible, and allow the Holy Spirit to teach us, we will know the difference between reality and the counterfeit. The Bible tells us that the Holy Spirit will guide us into all truth. *But when he, the Spirit of truth, comes, he will guide you into all truth (John 16:13).* The

REFLECTION
What helps you to recognize the difference between the real and the counterfeit Christian? How will the Holy Spirit guide you into all truth?

Holy Spirit convicts us in order to teach, correct and guide us into truth.

One day a friend gave me a candy bar. Little did I know that he had eaten the real candy bar and carefully replaced it with a piece of wood. When I opened the wrapper, I discovered his clever trick! Every Christian must examine himself to determine if his salvation is a present reality or if it is a counterfeit.

We are righteous through faith in God

How do we know we are right with God and not a counterfeit Christian? Romans 3:22 says we are righteous only through faith in Jesus Christ. *This righteousness from God comes through faith in Jesus Christ to all who believe....*

Righteousness is our right standing with God, being right with God. A *righteousness consciousness* means *being constantly conscious, or thinking about, our right standing with God through faith in Jesus Christ.*

Romans 4:3 tells us clearly...*Abraham believed God, and it was credited to him as righteousness. The* word *accounted* literally means *credited.* The Lord credits our account with righteousness when we believe Him! Imagine someone depositing money in your account at the bank each week. You say, "I don't deserve this." But your bank account would continue to grow whether you deserved it or not! That is exactly what God does. The Bible says that if we believe God, like Abraham, the Lord puts *righteousness* into our account! So, being right with God does not depend on our performance, it depends on our faith in Jesus Christ— our trust in Him.

When we begin to confess the truth of our righteousness by faith, do you know what happens? The Lord provides for our needs! *But seek first his kingdom and his righteousness, and all these things will be given to you as well (Matthew 6:33).* God provides for our needs because we are His children through faith in Jesus Christ. God makes us righteousness through faith in Jesus. God has accepted us. When we seek Him, He will provide for us!

REFLECTION
What is righteousness?
Describe how you have received righteousness by faith.

New Christians often make the mistake of relying too much on their feelings. One day they *feel* close to God and the next day they don't *feel* Him. We cannot trust our feelings. We have to trust the truth of the Word of God. When we are tempted to be discouraged or depressed, we must make the decision, in Jesus' name, to replace those thoughts with the thoughts that God thinks about us. See yourself as God sees you. Look at others as God looks at them. Seek first His kingdom and His righteousness, and the Lord will respond by adding all that you need!

Beware of having a sin consciousness

Some people have the opposite mentality of a righteousness consciousness; they have a "sin consciousness." When people have a sin consciousness they constantly are aware of, or thinking about, their tendency toward failure and sin. While it is true that by ourselves, we cannot obey God, the Bible says we can trust His competence (have faith in His strength to see us through). *Such confidence as this is ours through Christ before God. Not that we are competent in ourselves to claim anything for ourselves, but our competence comes from God. He has made us competent as ministers of a new covenant—not of the letter but of the Spirit; for the letter kills, but the Spirit gives life (2 Corinthians 3:4-6).*

It is only by God's competence that we are able to do anything. We have absolutely no chance of obeying God with our own strength. We must have faith in God's strength. Every time we look to ourselves to try to "pull ourselves up by our own bootstraps" we begin to live with a sin consciousness. Sin consciousness turns our thoughts inward. We depend on our own abilities and become proud when we succeed or feel like a failure when we do not succeed. Instead, we must look to Jesus, Who gives us strength and peace.

REFLECTION
What is a "sin consciousness"? Why is having a negative attitude a sign of weak faith? Is "pulling ourselves up by our own bootstraps" a biblical idea?

It's like this. If you're in the hospital and they take out your almost-ruptured appendix, what are you going to concentrate on? The pain? The stitches? Or are you going to say, "Praise God! The poison's being removed. I'm being healed in Jesus' name!" We choose to think of one or the other, the pain or the healing. If we keep our eyes on Jesus and on His righteousness, then God is free to allow the abundant life that He promised to permeate our lives.

I can promise you that if you're a child of God, and if there is an area in your life where you are sinning, the Lord will tell you. He loves you that much. He will tell you through His Word or He may bring people into your life to tell you. He will do whatever it takes to make sure that you know the truth. This way, you will look to Jesus and know you are "righteous in Him." When we understand this principle and begin to live in the righteousness of God, we begin to live a life of victory. Whenever we look to ourselves instead of to Jesus for our righteousness, we begin to experience confusion and discouragement.

Plant your righteousness seeds

Did you ever wake up on a holiday and find your alarm ringing in the morning at its normal time? You wake up and tell yourself you have to go to work, then you realize, "This is a holiday! I can sleep in!" You awaken to the truth.

The Bible encourages us to "awake to righteousness:" I can witness! I can be a man or woman of God! I can go to work and enjoy it! I can love my parents! I can raise a family for the Lord, regardless of my present circumstances! I can take a step of faith! I can be victorious! I am righteous through faith in Jesus Christ! You awaken to the God-given truth that you can live righteously and victoriously by the grace of God. *Awake to righteousness, and do not sin, for some do not have the knowledge of God...(1 Corinthians 15:34a NKJ).*

I once heard the story of a rescue operation of two men in a boat that had capsized. A helicopter dropped a rope and the first man held onto the rope to be pulled up into the helicopter. But the second man cried out, "Oh, don't do that! It's extremely dangerous to hang onto a rope tied to the bottom of a helicopter." Both men had a choice. They could either hang onto the rope and be pulled to safety or lose their lives. Either we trust God and receive His righteousness by faith instead of trusting in dead works, or die spiritually. That's how important this truth is. Righteousness through faith in Jesus is the only way out.

Again, I want to emphasize that righteousness through faith has nothing to do with the way we feel. It is based on the Word of God and His ability, not on us and our limited ability to "be good." Sometimes it takes time to see the results of living in righteousness by faith. It is like a certain kind of gigantic tropical species of bamboo plant. Initially, the new shoots grow slowly, but suddenly the growth rate increases rapidly and may reach nearly 60 cm (24 inches) per day![1]

So, do not give up. Plant your "righteousness consciousness seeds" and say, "I'm righteous by faith in Jesus." You may not feel any different, but you keep saying it because you know it is true. Faith comes by hearing, and hearing by

REFLECTION
What are some ways you can "awake to righteousness"? How is your thinking changed? When you confess the Word of God, what happens?

the Word of God (Romans 10:17). One day the Word of God is going to bear fruit in your life and it's going to grow and completely change your life.

Don't be afraid to talk to yourself. I talk to myself all the time. The Bible says David talked to himself; he *"encouraged himself in the Lord" (1 Samuel 30:6 KJV)*. Another time, in Psalms 103:1, we see David talking to himself, *"Praise the Lord, O my soul; and all my inmost being, praise his holy name!"* We should be doing the same thing. I encourage you to get up in the morning and say, "I am righteous through faith in Jesus. I am a man or woman of God. I can do all things through Christ who strengthens me today" (Philippians 4:13).

[1] "Bamboo," Microsoft® Encarta® Online Encyclopedia 2001, http://encarta.msn.com © 1997-2001 Microsoft.

Look to Jesus

DAY 7

Remember how Satan deceived Adam and Eve in the Garden? He continues to deceive and blind the minds of people today. The devil hates to see people put their trust and faith in the Lord. He knows that if he can get people to look at fear, poverty, disease, and their circumstances, they become defeated and depressed. Some days I don't spend enough time with God even though I know the Lord has called me to seek His face, read His Word, and look to Him. It is often at these times that the devil comes to me to say, "It's all over, because you failed. Now God can't use you."

Instead of listening to his lies, I immediately pray, "Lord, I believe what your Word says about me. I repent of 'missing the mark' today, and by your grace, Lord, I am going to be obedient to You."

There is a toy that you can find in some department stores. It's a big, tall toy on a heavy base. When you push it over, it always pops back up. That's the way God wants us to be as Christians. We need to say, "I will not listen to the lies of the devil. If I fall, I will get up in Jesus' name, and move on with my God."

REFLECTION
What are some ways the devil lies to you?
When God thinks about you, what is His will for you?

A man of God once said, "Look around, and get distressed. Look within, and get depressed. Look to Jesus, and be at rest." We must trust God in faith to truly please Him. The Lord has great plans for our lives according to Jeremiah 29:11. *"For I know the plans I have for you," declares the Lord, "plans to prosper you and not to harm you, plans to give you hope and a future."*

Yes, He is talking about you and me. Our God is thinking of us and cares about our futures!

CHAPTER 3

The Potent Mixture: Faith and the Word

KEY MEMORY VERSE

Consequently, faith comes from hearing
the message, and the message is heard
through the word of Christ.
Romans 10:17

How do we know the Bible is the true Word of God?

In this chapter, we will discover how faith and God's Word, the Bible, is a powerful mix to help us live the abundant life Christ wants to give us. But first, let's briefly look at why we believe the Bible is the true Word of God. Some of the many books today that claim to be the Word of God are the Koran, the Book of Mormon, the Bhagavad Vita and the Bible. Christians believe the Bible is the Word of God and the source of truth to live by. So what is the evidence proving the authority and divine origin of the Bible?

The Bible proclaims to be the Word of God. *All scripture is inspired by God (2 Timothy 3:16). Inspired* means *God-breathed.* The writers of scripture were supernaturally guided to write what God wanted written. *Holy men of God spoke as they were moved by the Holy Spirit (2 Peter 1:20-21).*

Jesus taught that the scripture is God's inspired Word even to the smallest detail. *I tell you the truth, until heaven and earth disappear, not the smallest letter, not the least stroke of a pen, will by any means disappear from the Law until everything is accomplished (Matthew 5:18).*

Although skeptics have tried to destroy the authority of the Bible, the Bible has remained the most well-known book in the history of the world and has proven itself true again and again. The Bible was written over a period of 1500 years, by over 40 different authors from all walks of life, in many different countries, addressing hundreds of issues, and yet remains unified in its message from God. The unity alone is an amazing proof of the divine inspiration and authority of the Bible.

REFLECTION
What did Jesus teach concerning the scripture as the inspired Word of God (Matthew 5:18)?

Mixing faith and the Word

We need to take God's Word and mix it with faith. Hearing God's Word alone will not change us, but (by faith) acting on it will! The book of Hebrews tells us that...*the message they heard was of no value to them, because those who heard did not combine it with faith (Hebrews 4:2).*

Combining God's Word with faith is a supernatural mix that causes something powerful to happen. It reminds me of epoxy glue. When the two ingredients of epoxy glue are mixed together, something powerful happens and you can bond together all kinds of materials with it.

When I was a young boy, I really wanted a chemistry set. My parents never got me one. I think they were afraid that I would blow the roof off the house! However, I improvised by making my own experiments. One day I mixed baking soda and vinegar and discovered they make a great explosion! Baking soda and vinegar by themselves are not explosive, but when you mix them, an explosive chemical reaction occurs.

In the same way, you can trigger a spiritual explosion in your life when you mix the Word of God with your faith and say, "I'm going to believe God's Word and act on it." True faith rises up in your heart and you experience the abundant life that Jesus promised. You are not basing your life on your own righteousness, but instead, on the righteousness that comes by faith in Jesus Christ and His Word.

One day an emotionally depressed woman came to a wise believer for advice. She explained that her daughter was involved in immorality. He gave her simple advice, "You need to start seeing yourself and your daughter as God sees you. Rather than being despondent about her situation, see her behind the cross of Jesus. Confess the truth of God's Word for her life."

A few months later, the woman and her daughter came back, beaming from ear to car. The woman explained: "I prayed and began to see my daughter from God's perspective. She had been living with a man who was not her husband, and one day she woke up so depressed that she decided to take her own life. But, first, she came home to see me. My family and I received her with joy. She received so much love from our family that she made a decision to give her life to Jesus. Why? Because we saw her behind the cross with the love eyes of Jesus." This family placed their faith in the Word of God instead of their feelings or circumstances. The Lord wants you and me to do the same.

REFLECTION

Have you ever experienced a spiritual explosion in your life? Give an example when you not only heard God's Word but also acted on it in faith.

Jesus and His Word are one

The best way to serve Jesus Christ and know His will for our lives is simply to live in obedience to His Word—the scriptures. You see, Jesus and His Word are one. Revelation 19:13 says...*his name is the Word of God.*

When I travel, my wife often leaves me notes in my luggage. I love to read her notes because it's the same as if she were talking to me. When God's Word tells me He loves me or commands me to do something, it is the same as if Jesus were speaking to me audibly in His own words. We can constantly live under the Lordship of Jesus by listening to what He says—as expressed in His Word. Jesus tells us, *The words I have spoken to you are spirit and they are life (John 6:63b).*

True Christians have chosen to live their lives in complete obedience to the Word of God. His words are spirit and life to us! The Bible leads us directly into God's will, and it keeps us from living according to our own desires instead of His desires. You need to read God's Word every day and confess Jesus Christ as your Lord so you can live in victory. God's Word renews your mind. *Do not conform any longer to the pattern of this world, but be transformed by the renewing of your mind. Then you will be able to test and approve what God's will is—his good, pleasing and perfect will (Romans 12:2).*

REFLECTION
How does the Bible lead us into God's will for our lives? How is God's Word renewing your mind today?

When we renew our minds daily with the Word of God and obey God's Word and the truth found there, it not only helps us to know Jesus better; it sets us free! When we obey the words that He has spoken to us in the scriptures and the words that He speaks to us by His Holy Spirit, we are obeying God. That is why the scriptures are so important.

If I feel like holding a grudge against someone and yet see in the scriptures that if I do not forgive others, God will not forgive me (Matthew 6:14,15), I come to a crossroads in my life. Either I choose my way or God's way. We must trust and obey God's Word to renew our minds and change us.

Release your faith by confessing the Word

You can release your faith by confessing God's Word with your mouth according to Romans 10:9-10. *That if you confess with your mouth, "Jesus is Lord," and believe in your heart that God raised him from the dead, you will be saved. For it is with your heart that you believe and are justified, and it is with your mouth that you confess and are saved.*

We are saved when we believe the truth from the Word of God in our hearts and confess it with our mouths. When we receive Jesus, we receive the gospel or *good news*. God's Word, the Bible, is filled with God's good news.

Being "saved" does not only mean that we go to heaven, as wonderful as that is. It also means we are being healed and set free inside. It means we can be set free emotionally, financially, mentally and in every other area of our lives. The key is to believe the Word and confess it so faith can mix with God's Word and release mighty miracles in our lives.

I thank God every day that I'm righteous through faith in Jesus Christ. I'm thankful for His Word, and I'm thankful for what He's done in my life. I know that I am right with God, not because of the good works that I do, but because of faith in Jesus Christ.

When I became a new Christian, I began to read the Word of God day by day. I started to think and act differently because my mind was being renewed by the Word of God. Faith rose up in me as a result of God's Word, just like the scriptures promise in Romans 10:17. *Consequently, faith comes from hearing the message, and the message is heard through the word of Christ.*

REFLECTION
Explain how you have released your faith in the past week.

See faith coming

I have a friend who served as a pastor in India for many years. He said, "In Eastern cultures, we see the Bible differently than you do. We see in pictures. We read in the scriptures that faith comes by hearing and hearing by the Word of God, and we really see faith coming! We confess it because God says it is so, and we see it coming with our spiritual eyes."

I believe the Lord wants us to see what happens when we take the Bible seriously and speak the truth to ourselves. We will "see faith coming." Most of the time, people wait to feel their faith with their emotions, but this is going about it backwards.

Imagine a train running down a track. Let's compare the engine that pulls the train to the *Word of God*. The next car is *our faith*. And the last car, the caboose, is our *feelings* or *our emotions*.

When we place our faith in the Word of God, our "feelings or emotions" will always follow like a caboose. However, if we place our faith in our feelings first, we will be frustrated and the enemy will begin to discourage us. We must place our faith in the Word of God first. Then the "feelings of faith" will follow. Faith is not a feeling. It is a mighty, living force released in our lives when we choose to hear and confess God's Word daily. *For the word of God is living and active. Sharper than any double-edged sword, it penetrates even to dividing soul and spirit, joints and marrow; it judges the thoughts and attitudes of the heart (Hebrews 4:12).*

REFLECTION

Describe a time in your life you "saw faith coming." What happens when you place your faith in feelings rather than the Word of God?

The Word of God causes us to begin to think like Jesus thinks. The Word of God releases the Lord's power so that we can know the difference between our own thoughts (in the soul) and the thoughts the Lord has placed in our spirits.

Meditate on God's Word

DAY 6

To grow spiritually, we must read and meditate on the Word of God each day. In this way, our minds become renewed. We must fill our minds with the truth of the Word of God, or we will be sidetracked by the philosophies of the world system around us that are completely against the truth of Jesus Christ. Exercising faith in God involves reading God's Word and obeying it.

How do we meditate on the Word of God? To *meditate* simply means *to roll something around over and over again in our minds.* Joshua 1:8 tells us, *Do not let this Book of the Law depart from your mouth; meditate on it day and night, so that you may be careful to do everything written in it. Then you will be prosperous and successful.*

Cows have multiple stomachs. They will fill their stomachs with grass, and then spend the rest of the day laying under a shade tree "chewing their cud." Food is passed from one stomach to the other in stages as they intermittently burp it up and chew it again. We could liken this process to meditating on the Word of God. We need to read the Word, and then write portions of it down and bring it back various times throughout the day to memorize it and meditate on it (chew on it!).

When I gave my life to Christ, I wrote down a verse of scripture that seemed to have special significance to me on an index card. Throughout the day, I pulled out the card to memorize it and meditate on its meaning. I

REFLECTION
What are some ways you meditate on God's Word?

literally "rolled around" God's Word in my mind until it became a part of me. During the first few years as a new Christian, I memorized hundreds of verses of scriptures this way.

There is a big difference between meditation on God's Word and the meditation practiced with some yoga techniques or by Hindu gurus and Buddhist monks. These religious leaders and various modern-day new age cults instruct their followers to meditate with one primary goal: *to empty their minds*. In this disconnection between the body and spirit or altered state of consciousness, a doorway to the occult is opened to the human soul. In sharp contrast, God's Word encourages us to *fill our minds* with (meditate on) the Word of God! As we do so, the Holy Spirit illuminates the Word of God to our minds, and we are changed.

Spiritual sowing and reaping

DAY 7

God has called you and I to sow His Word by praying in alignment with its truth and by speaking it to others. Jesus talked about sowers of God's Word in the Gospel of Mark saying, *The farmer I talked about is anyone who brings God's message to others...the good soil represents the hearts of those who truly accept God's message and produce a plentiful harvest for God—thirty, sixty, or even a hundred times as much as was planted...(Mark 4:14,20 TLB).*

When we sow the seed of the Word of God, God works through it to produce a supernatural spiritual crop. It may not happen the first day, or the first week, but it will happen.

As a young boy, I remember throwing a few watermelon seeds into our garden. Months later we had watermelons everywhere! When we sow the Word of God through prayer and by confessing the truth into our lives and into the lives of others, we will see a mighty crop, a bountiful harvest come forth for God.

You sow dynamic spiritual seeds into lives through prayer and encouragement every time you pray for loved ones or for yourself. Remember that God has promised He will produce a crop through the seeds that we sow.

While traveling with a young man who was not yet a Christian, I began to sow spiritual seeds into his life. I simply told him, "God has a call on your life and I believe you are going to be a man

REFLECTION

Describe a time you sowed spiritual seeds into someone's life. Did you see immediate results or not?

of God. God is going to use you." Months later he told me he received Christ into his life and reminded me of the "seeds of truth" that I sowed into his life months before.

The whole world is God's spiritual garden, and He wants to sow seeds of life everywhere we go. Let's plant spiritual seeds by faith into people's lives. Then we can do what farmers do every year— pray and expect the seeds to grow.

CHAPTER 4

We Can Live Victoriously

KEY MEMORY VERSE
...Christ lives in me. The life I live in the body,
I live by faith in the Son of God,
who loved me and gave himself for me.
Galatians 2:20b

There's a battle to be fought

Why do so many people seem to be disinterested in the things of God? Many do not believe in Jesus because they are spiritually blinded by the enemy. *And even if our gospel is veiled, it is veiled to those who are perishing. The god of this age has blinded the minds of unbelievers, so that they cannot see the light of the gospel of the glory of Christ, who is the image of God (2 Corinthians 4:3-4).*

Satan not only tries to hide the truth of the gospel from us, he is ready to do battle with us once we become Christians. The walk of the Christian is described as a spiritual warfare, and we must be equipped to fight. According to Ephesians 6:12, there is a battle being waged for our souls. This battle is not with people, but with the demons of hell. *For our struggle is not against flesh and blood, but against the rulers, against the authorities, against the powers of this dark world and against the spiritual forces of evil in the heavenly realms.*

Prayer and the declaration of the Word of God breaks down these demonic hindrances so that we can receive the Word of God and the life-giving conviction of the Holy Spirit. A friend and I went to pray for a man who had cancer. My friend, the man's believing wife and daughter-in-law had been praying for his salvation for many years, but he was unwilling to receive Christ. After entering his home, I felt impressed to share my testimony with him. About thirty minutes later, he was ready to receive Jesus Christ as the Lord of his life! We rejoiced, knowing that the true battle was won in prayer prior to that day by those who loved him. In prayer, his friend, wife and daughter-in-law had battled the evil forces that had spiritually blinded their loved one, allowing the light of the gospel to penetrate.

Unbelief comes from the devil and from all of his hoards of demonic angels. We live in a spiritual world and must fight spiritual battles. *Therefore put on the full armor of God, so that when the day of evil comes,*

REFLECTION
Describe a spiritual battle you fought and won recently. How did God's Word aid you?

you may be able to stand your ground...take...the sword of the Spirit, which is the word of God (Ephesians 6:13a,17b). The sword of the Spirit that we use to conquer the devil is the Word of God. As we learned in the last chapter, we mix the Word of God with faith and sow the seeds. God promises that we will get a good crop and be victorious in our battles.

Complete in spirit, soul and body

There is another battlefield: it is in our minds. My mind is bombarded with many thoughts every day, some not from God. It is important to understand that temptation is not sin because *every Christian is tempted.* Temptation becomes sin when we think about it and begin to allow it to gain control of our thoughts and our actions. How do we handle the wrong thoughts that come to our minds? We speak the Word of God and rebuke the devil in the name of Jesus. Then we go on, knowing that we are righteous by faith in Jesus Christ.

As Christians, we need to daily purify ourselves from every sin that threatens to contaminate us. The Bible teaches us that we are made up of body, soul and spirit. Before you were a Christian, your body, soul and spirit were polluted by sin. But as a believer, you are made holy. *May God himself, the God of peace, sanctify you through and through. May your whole spirit, soul and body be kept blameless at the coming of our Lord Jesus Christ (1 Thessalonians 5:23).*

If you and I sat down and talked face to face, you would not see all of me. What you would see is my body. My spirit is the part of me that communicates with God. My soul is a composite of my mind, my will, and my emotions.

Like me, you have the three aspects of spirit, soul and body. When we are born again by the Spirit of God, we receive Jesus as Lord and our spirits are instantly born again. We are brand-new inside. Do our bodies change? Absolutely. Look closely at people who are filled with Jesus, they have a sense of the Lord's peace on their countenance. They "glow" because of the Lord's presence and their faces shine with the glory of God.

What happens to the soul? The soul doesn't change instantaneously. It begins to be renewed as we read, hear and meditate on the Word of God. The Bible tells us to...*be transformed by the renewing of your mind. Then you will be able to test and approve what God's will is—his good, pleasing and perfect will (Romans 12:2).*

To a certain degree, we are all products of our past. We learned to think a certain way (man's way) about the main issues of life. The Word of God renews our minds to see life from *God's perspective* and reap the benefits that come with divine wisdom (see Joshua 1:8).

By meditating on the Word of God, we begin to see ourselves from the Lord's perspective instead of from our perspectives. A new Christian will find that his soul (mind, will and emotions) begins to catch up with what happened in his spirit when he received Jesus as his Lord. Gradually, he starts to "think like God" (he thinks according to the guidelines revealed in God's Word), instead of his past way of thinking.

When we lay our past (and present) before the Lord, His peace will stand guard at the door of our hearts and minds and change us. *And the peace of God, which transcends all understanding, will guard your hearts and your minds in Christ Jesus. Finally, brothers, whatever is true, whatever is noble, whatever is right, whatever is pure, whatever is lovely, whatever is admirable—if anything is excellent or praiseworthy—think about such things (Philippians 4:7-8).*

If we fix our minds on the holy things in life, God's peace will prevent the heartaches of this world from wrecking our lives. The Lord knows we are a work in progress, and He will change us daily—body, soul and spirit!

REFLECTION
What do you do when you are tempted to sin?
How is your body, soul and spirit being renewed?

DAY 3

You are a new creation

As soon as you are born again—you have received Jesus as Lord—a miracle has happened inside of you. You became a brand new person. You are a new creation in Jesus Christ. The Bible says in 2 Corinthians 5:17, *Therefore, if anyone is in Christ, he is a new creation; the old has gone, the new has come!*

An elephant becoming a butterfly would be no greater miracle! Yes, there is an indescribable miracle that happens inside of us as we live by faith in Jesus. Remember, putting our faith in Jesus means we cannot trust ourselves or our good works. In 2 Corinthians 1:9-10, Paul was imprisoned and in very dire circumstances. Still, he urged the Corinthian church to not trust in themselves but trust in God who alone has the power to deliver. *...That we might not rely on ourselves but on God, who raises the dead. He has delivered us from such a deadly peril, and he will deliver us. On him we have set our hope that he will continue to deliver us.*

Faith is believing and trusting in God and God alone. It's not a matter of "turning over a new leaf" or just changing some of our old ways of doing things. No, a miracle has happened inside. We

REFLECTION

Explain in your own words what it means to be "in Christ."
What is the evidence of being a new creation?

can know it has happened because God's Word says it has. We know by faith in the Word of God that we are new creations in Jesus Christ. Christianity is walking by faith, not by sight! We are righteous only by faith in Jesus Christ, and He makes us new day by day.

Set free!

DAY 4

When we join God's family, we are set free from the power of sin over our lives; we are set free from its guilt. Jesus tells us in John 8:31,32...*if you hold to my teaching, you are really my disciples. Then you will know the truth, and the truth will set you free.*

The first part of that verse says we must continue in God's Word—love it, keep it, and walk in it—and we shall know the truth and experience freedom. No one is truly free until the power of sin has been rendered inoperative as we consider ourselves dead to sin and alive to God. The Bible tells us that we are adopted into God's family. *For you did not receive a spirit that makes you a slave again to fear, but you received the Spirit of sonship. And by him we cry, "Abba, Father" (Romans 8:15).*

Every person living in sin is subject to fear because he is guilty! His conscience will trouble him. But a Christian does not have this fear because he has been adopted as a child into God's family (John 1:12, Ephesians 1:5, Galatians 4:5).

False guilt is something that feels like guilt but it is really just shame. It is the leftover negative feelings from our sinful past. False guilt causes us to hang on to our feelings of being dirty and sinful, even after we have confessed our sins and God has forgiven us. Before I received Jesus as my Lord, I experienced genuine guilt over my sins. Yet even after I received the Lord, the guilt continued although I was totally forgiven from God's perspective. Then I read 1 John 1:9 in God's Word, *If we confess our sins, he is faithful and just and will forgive us our sins and purify us from all unrighteousness.*

From that moment on, I stopped living by past experiences, feelings, and fears. I started living by the Word of God, and the guilt left. I knew I was forgiven because the

REFLECTION
In what ways has "the truth" set you free?

Bible told me so! I remembered that God had "removed my sins as far as the east is from the west" (Psalms 103:12). I was safe from all condemnation for my sins. It was as if they had not been committed at all. That is how freely God forgives when we place our trust in Him!

The devil condemns; God convicts

The devil will tell us that it is a long way back to God when we sin. He will try to make us believe that God will never use us again. But we now know better. If we sin, we must repent (we stop it and we change our direction). The Lord forgives us, and we start with a new, clean slate.

Sometimes restitution has to follow repentance. This is putting things right with people we have wronged. If someone repents from shoplifting, he needs to pay it back. Although he is forgiven the moment he confesses his sin, he needs to take a step of obedience and restore what was stolen. When Zacchaeus repented for running a crooked tax collection agency, he told the Lord he would restore four times what he stole (Luke 19:8-9).

Some time after I received Jesus Christ as my Lord, I was convicted by the Holy Spirit when I remembered I had deceived a classmate in high school. Another friend and I were gambling with him and had "rigged it" so that he always lost. I wrote to the classmate, explained what had happened and asked him for forgiveness, returning the money that I had taken from him, with interest. A few weeks later, I received a return letter saying he forgave me and thanking me for writing. I did not restore what I had taken so that I could be forgiven; I restored it because I *was* forgiven.

The devil condemns us, but God convicts us of our sin. What is the difference between the two? Condemnation brings doubt, fear, unbelief and hopelessness. Satan condemns us to bring us down and destroy our faith. God convicts us to restore us to righteousness and faith. He always corrects us to build us up, and His conviction always brings hope and a way of escape. *No temptation has seized you except what is common to man. And God is faithful; he will not let you be tempted beyond what you can bear. But when you are tempted, he will also provide a way out so that you can stand up under it (1 Corinthians 10:13).*

Don't accept condemnation from Satan or from other people. *Therefore, there is now no condemnation for those who are in Christ Jesus, because through Christ Jesus the law of the Spirit*

REFLECTION
Think about a time you have felt condemned rather than convicted of a sin. Explain the difference.

of life set me free from the law of sin and death (Romans 8:1 2).

Jesus Christ has made you free! You are free from the law of sin and death. He has made you righteous by faith in Him.

You can have a full life!

DAY 6

Christ wants to give us a full, abundant life, and He tells us so when He says...*I have come that they might have life, and that they may have it more abundantly (John 10:10 NKJ).*

The term *abundant life* is translated from the Greek word *zoe* which means *the very nature of God and source of life.* The abundant life then, is life filled with the very nature of God inside of us. This life is abundant in quantity and quality—overflowing life. That is the kind of life that God has prepared for us as His children.

Christ lives in us to help us live victoriously and fully. *Christ lives in me. The life I live in the body, I live by faith in the Son of God, who loved me and gave himself for me (Galatians 2:20b).* I keenly remember when this truth was made real to me while working on the family farm. I was herding livestock and frustrated by my lack of ability to accomplish the task. Then I prayed for God's wisdom rather than trusting in my own strength. As I confessed the truth of "Christ living in me," I was energized to complete my job! I received a clear realization that the Lord lived in me and wanted me to depend on His strength and His alone!

Do you want to know what the Lord's will is for your life? Of course you do! Trust completely that Jesus is in control of your life and wants to give you the strength you need to persevere. Begin to renew your mind daily with the Word of God, and you will discover the Lord's plans for your life. Our minds are like a painter's canvas, with God's Word the paint. God, the Holy Spirit, is like a paintbrush who wants to paint a clear picture concerning His will for our lives, but we need to have enough paint available for Him to draw us a clear picture.

Briefly, here are a few things to do to grow spiritually. We should worship God on a daily basis (John 4:23-24). We need to pray to Him and read the Bible. It is also important to worship with other Christians on a regular basis (Hebrews 10:24-25). We need to find a local church and develop relationships with the people there. In addition, we should share the gospel with others who need to hear (Matthew 28:19-20). When we do these things, we can expect our life-style to change. We will begin to experience the abundant life Jesus came to give us!

REFLECTION
Name some of the things you do that help you to experience an abundant life in Christ.

You are accepted!

Ephesians 1:6 tells us we are "accepted in the beloved" (God's family). When we are born again, we actually become a part of God's family! The Creator of the universe wants you and me to be in His family! 1 John 3:1 says, *How great is the love the Father has lavished on us, that we should be called children of God!*

Think of it! You really are a child of the living God when you receive Jesus Christ by faith. You are righteous! No matter what you have done today or yesterday, you are right with God as soon as you believe God's Word is true and say, "Lord, I know I'm righteous only because of my faith that You've given me—faith in Jesus Christ. Thank You, God, that I am righteous not by my works but by faith in Jesus Christ today!"

We all have a need to be accepted. I have felt misunderstood, left out and rejected many times in my life. In my first year at school, I was one of those kids who was usually the last one picked to play baseball with my schoolmates. It really hurt.

How about you? Can you remember times in your life when you felt all alone? Here is the good news. We are not alone! We can be secure in the fact that God loves us. When I realized that Jesus Christ accepted me just the way I was, a new security came into my life. And now, I can accept others, because I know that God has accepted me!

God has good plans for your life today. He wants you to reign in life through Jesus Christ because...*those who receive God's abundant provision of grace and of the gift of righteousness reign in life through the one man, Jesus Christ (Romans 5:17b).*

REFLECTION
Can you call God your "Father"?
Are you "reigning in life" through Jesus Christ?

Do not allow the enemy to get your focus off of Jesus and His righteousness. Refuse to be controlled by your feelings or circumstances. Rise up in faith and begin to reign in life through Jesus Christ and His righteousness! I have some good news for you: You don't have to wait. You can start today!

Works Vs. Faith

1. An elementary principle: Repentance from dead works

a. Let's look at the first of six elementary principles in Hebrews 6:1-2: **repentance from dead works**, faith toward God, baptisms, laying on of hands, resurrection of the dead and eternal judgment.

b. Salvation comes only through saving faith in Christ. We must repent from dead works (those "good deeds" will not get us to heaven!).

c. Even if we stumble in one point of the law of God, we are guilty (James 2:10).

2. True repentance or false repentance?

a. Godly sorrow accompanies true repentance
2 Corinthians 7:10

b. Repenting is "an inner change of mind resulting in an outward turning around."

c. False repentance is "repenting for any other reason except that God is worthy of our complete obedience."

Ex: Judas repented but did not change his mind or direction.

3. Good works vs. dead works

a. *Works* are good deeds we do. A *dead work* is any good deed we do to try to gain favor with God (Galatians 3:1-3,5).

b. We are saved through faith in Christ, we cannot trust our good works to get us to heaven (Ephesians 2:8-9).

Ex: Malaysian ritual (any religious works we think will bring us favor with God).

4. The futility of our works to save us

a. Even the best good works we perform to please God are like filthy rags compared to His goodness (Isaiah 64:6).

Ex: Beggar and king

b. We do not deserve it, but the Lord receives us as righteous.

5. God's perspective on good works

a. We should do good works, but not to try to earn God's favor. Ephesians 2:10

Ex: Boy hoeing garden. Mother loved him despite a poor job.

b. God empowers us to live the Christian life so we will want to act on the great love He bestows on us.

c. God's life in us produces good works/changed character.

6. True righteousness

a. We cannot establish our own righteousness by having a misdirected zeal for God (Romans 10:2-3).

Ex: Young football player heading in wrong direction.
Wrong currency in a foreign country.

b. We must be more than sincere; we must know the truth that right standing only comes through faith in Jesus Christ.

c. We will do good works but only because we have already been accepted by the Lord, not to try to be accepted by Him.

7. What is like a pile of rubbish?

a. Paul was an influential first century Christian, but he considered all he had done as a pile of garbage (Philippians 3:7-8) compared to knowing Christ.

b. We cannot trust our Christian background, training or credentials to make us acceptable to God.

c. We are accepted by trusting Jesus.

d. True repentance always goes before true faith.

e. We must repent of placing our faith in dead works and do an "about face" by placing our faith in God alone!

Faith in God

1. An elementary principle: Faith toward God

a. The second of six elementary principles in Hebrews 6:1-2 is "faith toward God": repentance from dead works, **faith toward God,** baptisms, laying on of hands, resurrection of the dead and eternal judgment.

b. Faith toward God produces a change in our hearts; it is believing first and then seeing (Hebrews 11:1).

c. Abraham "in hope believed" (Romans 4:18) long before he had a son.

d. Faith is a gift (Ephesians 2:8) and we each have a measure of faith (Romans 12:3).

2. We receive Jesus by faith alone

a. Faith is our first response to God (Hebrews 11:6).

b. Christ now lives inside us (Galatians 2:20) and enables us to live a supernatural life.

3. Put yourself to the test

a. People may look like Christians on the surface, but have no real spiritual life inside.

   Ex: Fake candy in empty wrapper.

b. Make sure we are genuine (2 Corinthians 13:5).

c. The Holy Spirit guides us to truth (John 16:13).

4. We are righteous through faith in God

a. How are we right with God? (Romans 3:22).

b. Righteousness is being right with God through faith in Christ.

c. The Lord credits our account with righteousness! Romans 4:3

d. We cannot trust our feelings. Trust God's Word.

5. Beware of having a sin consciousness

a. We cannot obey God on our own strength. If we try, we will have a sin consciousness (focus on our tendency toward sin).

b. However, we can trust God's competence. We must have faith in His strength to help us do anything.
2 Corinthians 3:4-6

c. We cannot "pull ourselves up by our own bootstraps!"

6. Plant your righteousness seeds

a. We must realize we are righteous and awaken to it.
1 Corinthians 15:34

Ex: Rescue operation (it's dangerous, but we have to trust the rope holds or remain behind and die)

b. Either we trust God and receive His righteousness by faith or trust dead works and die spiritually.

c. Takes time to see the results of living in righteousness.

Ex: Certain species of bamboo plant grows slowly, then the growth rate increases rapidly.

d. Encourage yourself in the Lord (1 Samuel 30:6).

e. You can do all things through Christ (Philippians 4:13).

7. Look to Jesus

a. Satan lies to us and tries to get us to look at our circumstances rather than God's Word.

b. Refuse Satan's lies and move on with God!

Ex: Toy with heavy base always pops up when pushed over.

c. God has great plans for us (Jeremiah 29:11) and cares about our future.

The Potent Mixture: Faith and the Word

1. How do we know the Bible is the true Word of God?
   a. The Bible proclaims to be the inspired Word of God.
   2 Timothy 3:16
   b. Writers of scripture were supernaturally guided to write what God wanted (2 Peter 1:20-21).
   c. Jesus taught that scripture is inspired to the smallest detail. Matthew 5:18

2. Mixing faith and the Word
   a. Hearing God's Word alone will not change us. Must combine it with faith (Hebrews 4:2).

   Ex: Like epoxy glue: the combination of ingredients creates powerful bond.
   b. Combine God's Word and faith and act on it.

3. Jesus and His Word are one
   Revelation 19:13
   a. Jesus speaks to us through His Word (John 6:63b).
   b. God's Word renews our minds (Romans 12:2).

4. Release your faith by confessing the Word
   a. Confessing God's Word with your mouth releases faith. Romans 10:9-10
   b. Faith comes from hearing the message of Christ. Romans 10:17
   c. A new Christian starts to think and act differently because his mind is renewed by God's Word.

5. See faith coming

Ex: Eastern cultures see in pictures. They visualize faith actually coming!

a. Place faith in God and feelings and emotions will follow.

Ex: Engine on a train (the Word of God) is first. Next car is faith and last car is feelings or emotions.

b. Faith is a living force released in our lives by placing our faith in God's Word (Hebrews 4:12).

6. Meditate on God's Word

a. Exercising faith in God involves meditating on God's Word and obeying it.

b. Meditate: to roll something around over and over again in our minds (Joshua 1:8).

Ex: Cows have multiple stomachs.

c. The difference between meditation on God's Word and meditation practiced by yoga techniques or Buddhists: they encourage emptying your mind; God's Word encourages you to fill your mind with the Word of God.

7. Spiritual sowing and reaping

a. Sow the seed of God's Word and produce a spiritual crop. Mark 4:14,20

Ex: Watermelon seeds in garden produce a bountiful crop.

Ex: Sow seeds of the truth in someone's life, they may come to Jesus.

b. Pray and expect the seeds to grow!

We Can Live Victoriously

1. **There's a battle to be fought**
   a. Satan tries to blind us to the truth (2 Corinthians 4:3-4).
   b. We are in spiritual warfare (Ephesians 6:12).
   c. Prayer and declaration of God's Word breaks down the barriers.
   d. Put on the armor of God (Ephesians 6:13,17) to fight the battle.

2. **Complete in spirit, soul and body**
   a. Another battlefield is in our minds. Our minds are bombarded with thoughts, some not from God.
   b. We need to daily purify ourselves (1 Thessalonians 5:23)—body, soul and spirit.
   c. Body: what you see when you look at me.
   d. Spirit: the part of you that communicates with God. Our spirits are instantly born again when we receive Jesus.
   e. Soul: does not change immediately. Begins to be renewed as we mediate on the Word of God (Romans 12:2).
   f. God's peace will stand guard at the door of our hearts and minds and change us (Philippians 4:7-8).

3. **You are a new creation**
   a. As soon as you receive Christ—you are a new creation. 2 Corinthians 5:17
   b. Faith is believing and trusting in God completely. 2 Corinthians 1:9-10

4. Set free!

a. We are set free from the power of sin over our lives—free from the guilt (John 8:31-32).

b. We are adopted into God's family (Romans 8:15).

5. The devil condemns; God convicts

a. When we sin, the devil will try to make us believe God will never use us again.

b. God forgives us and we start with a clean slate, but sometimes restitution must follow repentance. Zacchaeus repented and repaid four times what he stole (Luke 19:8-9).

c. Condemnation brings doubt, fear, unbelief.

d. Conviction brings hope and a way of escape.
   1 Corinthians 10:13

6. You can have a full life!

a. Christ came to give us abundant life (John 10:10).
   Abundant life means *the very nature of God.*

b. Christ lives in us and helps us live victoriously.
   Galatians 2:20

c. Things that can help us grow spiritually:
   Worship God (John 4:23-24)
   Pray and read the Bible, worship with other Christians. Hebrews 10:24-25
   Share the gospel with others (Matthew 28:19-20).

7. You are accepted!

a. We are loved and accepted in God's family.
   Ephesians 1:6; 1 John 3:1

b. You can reign in life through Jesus Christ
   Romans 5:17

Chapter 1
Works Vs. Faith
Journaling space for reflection questions

DAY 1 *Building a solid foundation in your Christian life involves under-standing what six principles? What does "repentance from dead works" mean?*

DAY 2 *What is the difference between true repentance and false repentance? What must be your only reason for repenting? What does godly sorrow lead to?*

DAY 3 *In efforts of trying to gain favor with God, what are some "dead works" people perform? How can you know your works are good and not dead?*

DAY 4 *Examine yourself—are you hanging onto some ragged dead works "just in case"? On what condition does God accept you?*

DAY 5 *If your own good works are not pleasing to God, how do you explain Ephesians 2:10? Why does God expect good works from you? What must be your only motivation for doing good works?*

DAY 6 *How do people try to establish their own righteousness? How can you know your "zeal for God" does not result in dead works?*

DAY 7 *Name some things Paul, the apostle, calls "rubbish"" that we often trust instead of trusting in God's righteousness. Is knowing Jesus personally the most important thing in your life?*

Chapter 2
Faith in God
Journaling space for reflection questions

DAY 1
What does faith produce?
According to Romans 12:3, where does faith come from?

DAY 2
How can you please God?
How can Christ live in you and you in Him?
In what ways is Christ living in you?

DAY 3
What helps you to recognize the difference between the real and the counterfeit Christian?
How will the Holy Spirit guide you into all truth?

What is righteousness?
Describe how you have received righteousness by faith.

What is a "sin consciousness"? Why is having a negative attitude
a sign of weak faith?
Is "pulling ourselves up by our own bootstraps" a biblical idea?

What are some ways you can "awake to righteousness"?
How is your thinking changed?
When you confess the Word of God, what happens?

What are some ways the devil lies to you?
When God thinks about you, what is His will for you?

The New Way of Living

Chapter 3
The Potent Mixture:
Faith and the Word
Journaling space for reflection questions

DAY 1 *What did Jesus teach concerning the scripture as the inspired Word of God (Matthew 5:18)?*

DAY 2 *Have you ever experienced a spiritual explosion in your life? Give an example when you not only heard God's Word but also acted on it in faith.*

DAY 3 *How does the Bible lead us into God's will for our lives? How is God's Word renewing your mind today?*

Biblical Foundations

Explain how you have released your faith in the past week.

Describe a time in your life you "saw faith coming."
What happens when you place your faith in feelings rather than the
Word of God?

What are some ways you meditate on God's Word?

Describe a time you sowed spiritual seeds into someone's life.
Did you see immediate results or not?

Chapter 4
We Can Live Victoriously
Journaling space for reflection questions

DAY 1

Describe a spiritual battle you fought and won recently.
How did God's Word aid you?

DAY 2

What do you do when you are tempted to sin?
How is your body, soul and spirit being renewed?

DAY 3

Explain in your own words what it means to be "in Christ." What is
the evidence of being a new creation?

DAY 4

In what ways has "the truth" set you free?

DAY 5

Think about a time you have felt condemned rather than convicted of a sin. Explain the difference.

DAY 6

Name some of the things you do that help you to experience an abundant life in Christ.

DAY 7

Can you call God your "Father"? Are you "reigning in life" through Jesus Christ?

Daily Devotional Extra Days

If you are using this book as a daily devotional, you will notice there are 28 days in this study. Depending on the month, you may need the three extra days' studies given here.

DAY 29 — Effects of Righteousness

Read Isaiah 32:17 and write down the effects of righteousness. Does this mean in this life or only in the eternal life to come? (See Isaiah 9:7) If you don't have peace in your life, what should you do?

DAY 30 — Source of Strength

Read John 15:5 and Philippians 4:13. What is the connection between the two verses? Where do you get your strength? How? Is there any life possible in the branch if it is cut from the vine? How do you draw strength from the Vine?

DAY 31 — Blessings of the Righteous

Read Proverbs 10:6; 10:16 and 10:24. Write out the results of righteousness in these three verses. Now skim over chapters 10-14 of Proverbs and count the blessings of righteousness.
Is any of this possible without the righteousness of Christ in your life?

Coordinates with this series!

Biblical Foundations for Children

Creative learning experiences for ages 4-12, patterned after the *Biblical Foundation Series*, with truths in each lesson. Takes kids on the first steps in their Christian walk by teaching them how to build solid foundations in their young lives. by Jane Nicholas, 176 pages: $17.95 ISBN:1-886973-35-0

Spiritual Fathering & Mothering Seminar

Practical preparation for believers who want to have and become spiritual parents. Includes a manual and the book *The Cry For Spiritual Fathers & Mothers*.

Effective Small Group Ministry Seminar

Developing strategy for successful cell groups. For cell leaders and pastors. Includes a *House To House* book and a seminar manual.

Youth Cell Ministry Seminar

Learn the values behind youth cells so cell ministry does not become just another program at your church. For adult and teen leaders!

New House Church Networks Seminar

Learn how new house churches (micro-churches) are started, kept from pitfalls, and work with the rest of the body of Christ.

Elder's Training Seminar

Based on New Testament leadership principles, this seminar will equip elders to provide protection, direction and correction in the local church. Includes *The Biblical Role of Elders in Today's Church* book and a manual.

Church Planting Clinic

Designed to help you formulate a successful strategy for cell-based church planting. For those involved in church planting and those considering it. Includes a *Helping You Build Cell Churches* Manual.

Counseling Basics Seminar
for Small Group Leaders

This seminar takes you through the basics of counseling, specifically in small group ministry. Includes a comprehensive manual.

Fivefold Ministry Seminar

A seminar designed to release healthy, effective fivefold ministry in the local church. Includes a *Helping You Build Cell Churches* Manual.

Marriage Mentoring Training Seminar

Trains church leaders and mature believers to help prepare engaged couples for a strong marriage foundation by using the mentoring format of *Called Together*. Includes a *Called Together* Manual.

Seminars held at various locations throughout the US and Canada. For complete brochures and upcoming dates:

Call 1-800-848-5892
www.dcfi.org   email: info@dcfi.org